PRECIOUS MOMENTS

My Forever Friend

_____

GIVEN TO

_____

OCCASION

_____

DATE

But the fruit of the Spirit is love, joy, peace,
longsuffering, kindness, goodness, faithfulness,
gentleness, self-control.

Galatians 5:22-23

When you feel that certain sadness creeping over your soul, they care. When
good news fills your heart with gladness, they share your smile with you.
And when you need a listening ear, a word of encouragement or advice, they
are always there. They are God's precious gift to you—your best friends,
your soul mates, your friends for life.

My Forever Friend is a tribute to those special people in our lives that fill the
role of faithful friends. Featuring Sam Butcher's beloved PRECIOUS
MOMENTS® characters, *My Forever Friend*
depicts the blessed art of friendship, with
inspirational Scriptures alongside heart-
warming scenes of service and affection.
Together, the illustrations and verses point
not only to the bond we share with loved
ones here, but also to Jesus, our forever
Friend, who loves us with a love deeper than
any found on earth. May this book encourage you to draw strength from Him as you
continue to be a best friend to others.

The fruit of the Spirit
is love, joy, peace,
longsuffering, kindness,
goodness, faithfulness,
gentleness, self-control.

Galatians 5:22-23

"A new commandment
I give to you,
that you love one another;
as I have loved you,
that you also love one another."

John 13:34

A man who has friends
must himself be friendly,
But there is a friend
who sticks closer
than a brother.

Proverbs 18:24

Through love serve one another.
For all the law is fulfilled
in one word, even in this:
"You shall love your
neighbor as yourself."

Galatians 5:13–14

A friend loves
at all times,
And a brother is
born for adversity.

Proverbs 17:17

Be kindly affectionate
to one another with
brotherly love, in honor
giving preference
to one another.

Romans 12:10

She opens her mouth
with wisdom,
And on her tongue
is the law of
kindness.

Proverbs 31:26

"Greater love has
no one than this,
than to lay down one's
life for his friends."

John 15:13

Ointment and perfume
delight the-heart,
And the sweetness of
a man's friend gives
delight by hearty counsel.

Proverbs 27:9

Let us pursue the things which make for peace and the things by which one may edify another.

Romans 14:19

Behold, how good
and how pleasant it is
For brethren to dwell
together in unity!

Psalm 133:1

This is
my beloved,
And this is my friend.

Song of Solomon 5:16

Let all
that you do
be done with love.

1 Corinthians 16:14

I thank my
God upon every
remembrance
of you.

Philippians 1:3

I will never leave you nor forsake you.

Hebrews 13:5

It is one thing to know your friend. It is quite another to be known by the God of the universe. David caught a glimpse of this incredible union between Savior and sinner when in Psalm 139:1-3 he says, "O LORD, You have searched me and known me. You know my sitting down and my rising up; You understand my thought afar off. You comprehend my path and my lying down, and are acquainted with all my ways."

God does bless us with beautiful friendships here on earth to encourage us along the way, as well as provide an outlet of ministry to others. But the greatest gift of friendship is found in Jesus, who knows our every thought, our every word, and our every deed. He even knows the number of hairs on our heads! When we think we are in a place where no one can reach us, God can—because He sees us and knows us better than we know ourselves. Best of all, He loves us with an unselfish, unending love. His friendship never wavers, never fails, and fills our souls with gladness both now and forever.